ALL ANDORRA

Editorial Escudo de Oro, S.A.

At Sant Julià de Lòria, visitors are greeted by a few
patriotic words of welcome.

ESTEU EN TERRA ANDORRANA.
BENVINGUTS.

You are in Andorra. Welcome. With these words, all those entering Andorra in peace, with no distinction of race, colour or creed, are warmly welcomed by the people of the Valleys of Andorra into a land where all is peace. A landscape of superlative beauty is spread out before the visitor. From the idyllic valleys with their charming villages and enchanting Lombard Romanesque churches, to the soaring white mountain peaks — a paradise for winter sportsmen —, and the murmuring banks of the rivers' rushing waters, flanked by age-old leafy trees, Andorra is like a divine gift contemplating itself in the shining mirror of its splendid lakes. It is also a land of friendly, hospitable people who have made Andorra a haven of peace and happiness.

THE VALLEYS OF ANDORRA:
A MAGIC WORLD OF SNOW AND SUN

The Valleys of Andorra are situated at the heart of the Pyrenees, and extend, like a delightful, endless song of nature, over an area of 464 square kilometres of incomparably beautiful countryside in the Central and Eastern Pyrenees. Bounded — but not in any way restrained — by its frontiers with friendly Spain and France, Andorra is an oasis of peace and freedom, a land open to a warm life full of fellow-feeling, kindly enhancing the life of man in the years that lie ahead.

It is an unusual and secluded area, full of the marvels of nature. First, there are the high snow-capped mountains, soaring ever upwards into the skies — the peaks of Envalira, Siguer, Medacorba, Coma Pedrosa, Pla de l'Estany (the highest point in Andorra, at 2,951 metres), Pic de Llops, Pic de Montmalús, Bony de les Neres, Tristaina, La Rabassa, Setúria, dels Isards, Casamanya and l'Estanyó, altogether some 65 in total. Then there are the bubbling, cascading rivers, winding through this entire area of massive, imposing mountain ranges, rivers like the Valira d'Orient, the Valira del Nord, and the Gran Valira. There are the dream-like lakes — Engolasters,

Andorra's former coat of arms, possiby 14th century, at the Casa de la Vall.

View of Lake Xuclar.

those of the Vall d'Incles, of Tristaina and of Els Pessons —, the leafy woods, the country lanes and the idyllic valleys; any description of such vast, varied beauty can only be a pale reflection of the dazzling reality. It has to be seen at first hand, the spirit soaked in its charming atmosphere.

These mountains and valleys are the home of many wild animals, including eagles, vultures, woodcock, the white partridge, squirrels, wild boar, otters, foxes, wild cats, the ''isard'' — a goatlike antelope of the Pyrenees —, rabbits and hares. The abundant plant life includes rhododendrons, carnations, junipers, blue lilies, strawberries, raspberries, water-lilies, and snow-drops. Most interesting is the ''Gran-dalla'', a flower with six petals symbolising the

formerly six, though now there are in fact seven, municipalities or parishes of Andorra.

Andorra's climate is characteristically calm and stable, the matchless blue of its skies rarely marred by clouds, and often illuminated by a splendid, almost Mediterranean, sun. All these gifts of nature combine to make Andorra an enchanting haven of irresistible charm.

These valleys are thought to have been inhabited since the earliest times. To support this claim, there are the finds of the ''Balma de la Margineda'': pottery, beads and other objects from the Neolithic Age, and the Bronze Age relics found in the villages of La Serra d'Enclar and Cedre. The rock tomb of the ''Balma de la Margineda'', the cave paintings of the

"Roca de les Bruixes", the stone carvings of Ordino, the carved slates of Monalerí and the dolmen at Encamp also provide powerful archaeological evidence of prehistoric life in Andorra.

It is true that the Celts, the Iberians, the Andosins — a prehistoric tribe mentioned in Polybius' chronicles of their battles with Hannibal — the Vandals, the Alans, the Goths and the Arabs all penetrated the Valleys to the war-like sound of trumpets, but they left behind them no more than the mere echo of their passage. When, we may then ask, did the hour of history really sound clearly for Andorra? It has been claimed that the historical baptism of the country was the "Carta de Fundació d'Andorra", given by Charlemagne to his son, Louis I the Pious, preserved in the Principality Archives, but many believe this document to be apocryphal. However, there seems to be no doubt that for a time the Carolingians ruled over the Valleys, and that this authority later passed into the hands of the Counts of Urgell, who then gave the territory to the Bishop of Urgell. In the 12th century, the bishop of that time placed the diocese under the protection of the lords of Caboet, but at the beginning of the 13th century the Bishops of Urgell came into conflict with the Counts of Foix. A turbulent period of bloody strug-

La vall d'Envalira.

The Envalira Valley.

gle ensued, ending in 1278 when a treaty delimitating their respective jurisdictions was signed by Roger-Bernard III, Count of Foix and Pere d'Urtx, Bishop of Urgell, in the presence of Pere III of Aragon. A further treaty or ''Pareatge'' was signed under the authority of a bull of Martin IV. These historical agreements between the civil and ecclesiastical powers, made with the full approval of the people of Andorra, constitute the origins of the pact in force in Andorra to this very day.

In the 15th century, the Bishop co-prince, with the agreement of the other co-prince, the Count of Foix, conceded the Andorrans the right to manage their own affairs through the ''Consell de la Terra'', whose members were freely elected by the people. This Land Council was the forerunner of the present-day ''Consell General de les Valls'' (General Council). The Bishops of Urgell have retained their rights in Andorra to the present day, but, due to a succession of marriages, the rights of the Counts of Foix passed

Some specimens of the rich fauna of Andorra.

first to the Crown of Navarre and then to that of France, whose monarchs confirmed the privileges of the Principality in a number of charters. As a result of the situation brought about by the French Revolution, there was a rupture in relations between Andorra and France from the end of the 18th century to the beginning of the 19th. However, the ''Consell General'', desiring the restitution of the former Constitution, petitioned Napoleon, who reestablished normal conditions by a decree in 1806.

Scenery and the great Lake ''Els Pessons''.
The Grandalla (''Narcissus poeticus''), national emblem
of Andorra, with its six petals corresponding to the
formerly six, now seven, Parishes.

Some examples of the flora of Andorra.

During the first Carlist Civil War, differences arose between Andorra and the Bishop of Urgell, and on the 7th of March, 1842, the "Consell General" agreed that tithes should be replaced by a tax of 1,860 Barcelona pounds, of which 1,140 should go to the Bishop and 120 to each of the six municipalities.

The rights and privileges of Andorra having been acknowledged by General Prim in 1868, relations with Spain continued smoothly, but there were disagreements between the Andorrans themselves over a casino, finally resolved by the Treaty of Pont dels Escalls in 1881 and the elections of 1885.

After a long period of peace and progress, further troubles arose in 1933. A Russian, Boris Skossyreff, with the help of a group of councillors, attempted to proclaim himself King of Andorra, but, finally, he left the Valleys. On June 10th of the same year, the "Tribunal de Corts" (Law Court) dismissed the "Consell General", and a detachment of French gendarmes was brought in because of the situation caused by a group of Andorran patriots. They left at the end of the summer, though, and the electoral system was reformed. All males over 25 could vote, and those over 30 were elegible for election. This system lasted until 1971, when a group of young people claimed and won the right for both men and women to vote at 21 and to be eligible for election at 25.

Be that as it may, to ask an Andorran who the sovereign of Andorra is, is to receive the reply, ''The People''. The people are the only sovereign because power and authority comes from them. They are represented by the directly-elected permanent body known as the ''Consell General'' and by the municipalities. The historic institution of the co-princes remains, but now at the service of this democratic, independent community, providing the protection asked for by the Andorrans. Andorra maintained a strict neutrality during both the Spanish Civil War and the Second World War. Increasingly prosperous, Andorra has continued to progress until it has become the idyllic country of the present, without doubt one of the world's most attractive tourist resorts.

With its rich variety of plants, Andorra can be considered one of Europe's botanic gardens.

The Andorran coat of arms, on the Casa de la Vall.

POLITICAL INSTITUTIONS

Andorra has a unique form of government, known as the Coprincipality.

The "Consell General", or General Council, is the governing body of Andorra. It is the federal organ of the seven municipalities of Andorra, and is presided over by two officers, known respectively as the Syndic and Under-Syndic. The "Consell" is made up of 28 Councillors, four for each municipality, elected by secret direct universal suffrage every four years. These Councillors elect the Syndic and Under-Syndic, posts which may be held by any Andorran citizen, whether a member of the "Consell' or not. The "Consell" is the legislative body and also collects and distributes indirect taxes in the municipalities — there being no direct taxation in Andorra — and deals with general affairs. The "Consell" elects a Head of Government, who in turn appoints ministers, and submits a political programme to the approval of the "Consell General". The Government exercises executive power.

The two Princes, the Bishop of Urgell and the President of the French Republic, as heir of the former Counts of Foix, through two representatives known as "Veguers" or magistrates, take care of security and public order, and also judge court cases against the administration.

The Princes also have two permanent delegates, one who resides with the Bishop-prince in the Bishop's Palace at La Seu d'Urgell, and the other, the Prefect of the Eastern Pyrenees, in Perpignan. These delegates, acting jointly, settle administrative disputes and have some legislative, though not administrative powers, since it is the "Consell General" that holds the "poder de la terra", or administrative power.

Justice is carried out by the following bodies: in criminal law, the "Tribunal de Corts", a lower and appeal court rolled into one, whose verdict is binding, composed of an Appeals Judge, the two "Batlles" or Justices of the Peace, the two Notaries and, since 1976, barristors and the Public Prosecutor. Previously, the latter two could not appear before the courts, and defendants were represented by "Parladors", that is to say "speakers" or advocates, who were members of the "Consell General".

In civil law, there are three courts. The first is presided over by the "Batlles" or Justices of the Peace, Andorrans elected by the system known as "Setena", where the "Consell General" presents a list of seven candidates to the Princes, who choose two. The appeal court is presided over by the Appeals Judge, who is chosen alternatively by the Princes for a term of five years. The third court is the "Tribunal Superior de la Mitra" and Perpignan

— the High Court of the Bishopric and of Perpignan. There is no united births, marriages and deaths register in Andorra, and this is replaced by the Church Register. Nor are there land or mortgage records, but instead notarial registers, having full legal effect, and compiled by the two "Notaris" of Andorra.

Local administration is carried out by the "Parròquies" or "Comuns" — parishes or municipalities. There are two "Cònsols" or mayors per municipality, the senior and the junior, who are assisted in their work by their councillors — "Consellers del Comú". Some of the municipalities — divided into districts or "Quarts" corresponding to villages or hamlets — are administratively autonomous.

Andorra's unique democratic institutions are a model of political dexterity and wise diplomatic adaptation.

Council Chamber of the "Consell General", in the Casa de la Vall.

EL PAS DE LA CASA

A village situated on the border with France, and whose name, meaning "the pass by the house", has as its origin the shepherd's hut that was a landmark for travellers fording the River Ariège at that point. El Pas de la Casa is a paradise for winter sports enthusiasts — in fact it has been used as the venue for the European Championships — and is a most attractive tourist centre. Among its sports facilities are its ski slopes and ski lifts taking one at breath-taking heights to Coll Blanc, Grau Roig-Coll Blanc, Font Negra, Costa Redona and Solana, offering spectacular views of the valley and the mountains. Lake Font Negra is the source of the River Ariège, which flows into the Garona.

View of El Pas de la Casa.

Overall view and part of El Pas de la Casa.

Horses grazing at the Envalira Pass, and views of El Pas de la Casa.

*Two views of the
Envalira Pass.*

Lake Font Negra, at
El Pas de la Casa.

Lake ''Els Pessons''.

The Envalira Valley, with the ''Cercle dels Pessons'' in the background.

Lake ''Els Pessons''.

RANSOL

A small village situated at a height of 1,745 metres, from which there are beautiful panoramic views. There is a Romanesque church — reconstructed — at Ransol, and various old, typically Andorran, houses.

The Incles Valley.

St. Bernard pups.

Two views of Ransol.

The 12th-century Romanesque Church of Sant Joan de Caselles, Canillo.

Sant Joan de Caselles: stucco high relief of Christ surrounded by frescoes. Above the arms of the cross, there are the sun and the moon, and below, Longinus and Stefanton. This 12th-century work is framed by a painted frieze. The paintings could be the work of the Master of Argolell.

Overall view of Canillo.

The well-known ''Cross of the Seven Arms''.

CANILLO

The first, and most northerly, municipality of Andorra, lying on mountain slopes at a height of 1,531 metres. This is a picturesque, typically rural village, through which runs a surging stream. The delightful alleys and charming houses with their rustic wooden balconies and ancient wrought iron window grilles make up the evocative, medieval character of the town.

The area dominated by the popular *Molí Vell* is also

View of Canillo.

Waterfall at Canillo.

of great interest. A recommended excursion from Canillo is to the Church of Sant Joan de Caselles, considered a masterpiece of Andorran Romanesque. The present building — nave and bell tower —, is 12th-century, although features of an older construction remain. Its beautiful, harmonious bell tower consists of three storeys, with graceful double windows on the upper two storeys, and walls thicker than those of the nave. The church is entered through the porch, probably 15th-century, situated in the north side of the nave. The paintings of the interior are 12th-century, and represent just one theme, that of the Crucifixion.

Canillo also has a magnificent sports complex, the ''Palau de Gel d'Andorra''. The skating rink is the biggest in Southern Europe, the only one of maximum Olympic dimensions (30-60 metres). The ''Ice Palace'' is situated at 1,564 metres above sea level, it can seat 1,600 and is equipped with the most modern and comfortable facilities, swimming pool and solarium, squash courts, cinema, bar and restaurant, games room and, 50 metres away, another building with gymnasium, tennis courts and a sauna.

PRATS

A picturesque little village of pretty grey houses, overlooked by the Church of Sant Miquel, with its double-arched porch. Sant Miquel is the only Andorran church containing Gothic features, though the apse is Romanesque.

On the footpath between Canillo and Prats there is the famous *Creu de les Set Branques*, or ''Cross of Seven Arms''.

Archway at the entrance to the church at Canillo.

MERITXELL

The thousand-year old shrine has been called "the Lourdes of Andorra" because of its popularity. On the 8th of September — a Bank Holiday in the Valleys of Andorra — a large crowd of worshippers gathers around it. According to tradition, the statue of Our Lady of Meritxell was found by a group of Christians making their way from Encamp to Canillo, in the middle of winter, among some plants which were, miraculously, in flower. They took it to Canillo, where it disappeared mysteriously, to be found once more, among the flowering plants, in the same place. It was taken, this time to Encamp, where it disappeared again. It was decided to build the Shrine of Our Lady of Meritxell in the place where the statue had been found, and this monument has become the religious symbol of Andorra, the subject of numerous, passionately patriotic, songs of praise, for example, this verse:

The reredos of the Shrine of Our Lady of Meritxell.

Statue of Our Lady of Meritxell.

*The Shrine of Our
Lady of Meritxell.*

Les Bons.

The Romanesque Church of Sant Romà, Les Bons
(Encamp).

Quan l'infidel s'afanyava
contra Crist amb gran furor,
l'aspra muntanya ocultava
vostra imatge, ric tresor.
Mes el Cel volgué mostrar-vos
com un sol formós i clar.

The original statue of Our Lady of Meritxell, portrayed holding the Child Jesus in Her arms, was kept in a niche behind the altar. It was a beautiful old Romanesque polychrome wood carving. However, it was destroyed in a devastating fire in 1972, when only the remains of the original chapel were saved. A new shrine was built near to the burnt ruins, opened on the 8th of September 1976. The new shrine is of modern design, the work of the architect Ricard Bofill.

LES BONS

A small village standing on the banks of the River Valira, of great personality. Dominated by the Church of Sant Romà, one of the oldest in Andorra, Les Bons forms a pretty picture, with its typical alleys and the ruins of an old castle once belonging to the counts of Foix.

The church was consecrated in 1163, and its nave, with a narrower adjoining presbitery, is divided by main arches into three spaces. It has a semicircular apse with a series of Lombard arches on the outside, and a porch added at a later date. The church was decorated with frescoes attributed to the Master of Santa Coloma, now kept in the Museum of Catalan Art.

Overall view of Encamp.

LA MOSQUERA

A small village situated next to Encamp, on the left-hand side of the Valira, La Mosquera is a dynamic commercial centre with an attractive residencial area. Near to it is El Tremat, with its typical houses.

ENCAMP

The second-oldest of the seven municipalities of Andorra, after Canillo. It has a pretty church with a noteworthy Romanesque bell tower, altered in different periods.

Encamp is to be found in the large and lovely Valira Oriental Valley, at the foot of the slopes of Bony de les Neres, almost in the geographical centre of Andorra, at an altitude of 1,226 metres. The mountains surrounding Encamp are charming, adorned by lush green pastures.

A worthwhile excursion is to Els Cortals, a picturesque village which is only inhabited during the time of the tobacco harvest, at three kilometres from Encamp. Very close, at the top of the valley, one can see the humble outline of the pre-Romanesque Chapel of Sant Jaume dels Cortals. When in this area, it is not uncommon to suddenly spot a trout-fisher or a hunter of mountain goat.

The Church of Sant Miquel, which contains Romanesque features, at La Mosquera, (Encamp).

VILA

A hamlet beside the main road at the foot of the slopes of Bony de les Neres, Vila is made up of a group of typically Andorran houses and the small Romanesque Chapel of Sant Romà.

A panoramic view of Encamp.

Two views of Lake Engolasters. Situated at an altitude of 1,616.50 metres, it is Andorra's biggest lake, measuring 800 × 300 metres.

SANT MIQUEL D'ENGOLASTERS

The Church of Sant Miquel is to be found not far from Lake Engolasters, one of Andorra's most beautiful lakes, surrounded by pleasant woods at an altitude of 1,616 metres. The superb 12th-century Lombard bell tower rises up to an altitude of 1,500 metres, standing out as a unique architectural landmark amidst the spectacular countryside. This spot was once inhabited, as is recorded by two documents, dated 1162 and 1176 respectively.

Besides the bell tower, under the eaves of which there are some grotesque carvings (a human head and that of an eagle have been identified), the Romanesque apse, the small portico and the large Lombard windows are also to be noted in the church. The interior of this charming building was once decorated by some interesting Romanesque frescoes, work of the Master of Santa Coloma, which can now be seen in the Museum of Catalan Art. However, the original paintings were painstakingly reproduced here by specialists, a work inaugurated in 1981.

The 12th-century Romanesque Church of Sant Miquel d'Engolasters.

Les Escaldes and Andorra la Vella.

LES ESCALDES

This place takes its name from the sulphurous waters which rise from the bowels of the earth. The thermal springs reach a maximum temperature of 61°C and are used to heat many houses in the district. Les Escaldes lies to the north of Andorra la Vella in a luxuriant and fertile region. It is not only a spa and tourist centre but also a place of commercial and industrial activity of the greatest importance within the Principality.

The town of Les Escaldes extends along both sides of the main road and, with its modern buildings and very cosmopolitan way of life, it lends a splash of vivid colour to the surrounding countryside. Among its noteworthy monuments are the beautiful Gothic cross, which stands in the old square of Les Escaldes, and the neo-Romanesque church of Sant Jaume with a decorated Lombard belfry, a silhouette which stands out against the modern buildings nearby. In 1978 Les Escaldes-Engordany became the seventh municipality of Andorra.

Overall view of Les Escaldes-Engordany.

Les Escaldes:
Charlemagne avenue
by night.

Centre Termolúdic
Caldea.

Plaça dels Coprínceps, Les Escaldes-Engordany.

View of Les Escaldes-Engordany.

Les Escaldes: the square and avenue named after Charlemagne (Plaça and Avinguda de Carlemany).

Andorra la Vella.

View of Les Escaldes-Engordany and Andorra la Vella.

ANDORRA LA VELLA

The capital of Andorra, its fifth municipality, and its largest centre of population, Andorra la Vella is situated in the centre of a beautiful, fertile valley at the foot of the Serra d'Enclar, facing the ''Pic de Camp Ramonet''. At an altitude of 1,029 metres, it is the highest capital in Europe, occupying a privileged position overlooking the wide plain of the River Valira, not far from where Andorra's three main rivers meet.

The word *Vella*, as applied to the name of the city, has been wrongly translated to mean ''old'' when in reality it is derived from the word *vela*, meaning ''city''. *Vella*, therefore, by describing the capital as a city, distinguishes it from the rest of the country. Andorrans are, rightly, proud of their capital. It is a place of distinctive architectural and human personality, with a charming cosmpolitan air. Its most important and busy street is the Avinguda de Meritxell, the bustling heart of Andorra la Vella, with its enticing shop-windows, its *boutiques* overflowing with all manner of goods, its excellent restaurants and its modern hotels. Most of the Principality's public offices and institutions are to be found in the Pui quarter. It is a real pleasure to wander around the streets of this area, and also a risk, thanks to the temptation of the goods displayed in every shop win-

Overall view of Andorra la Vella.

Les Escaldes: Avinguda de Carlemany.

Plaça del Poble, Andorra la Vella.

dow. There are magnificent leather goods, an incredible variety of cigars and cigarettes, the finest French and Spanish wines, bottles of whisky and brandy and much more, their moderate prices making them even more attractive. Besides the Pui quarter and the beautiful Plaça del Bisbe Benlloch, throughout the length and breadth of Andorra la Vella there are many other enchanting nooks and typical squares allowing views of the mountains, the valley or the river which form the town's spectacular natural setting. To look across the snow-covered countryside from any of the capital's marvellous vantage points is to be won over by the magic of Andorra, and one might

Meritxell Avenue, Andorra la Vella.

Les Escaldes-Engordany and Andorra la Vella.

A sculpture by Viladomat, at the entrance courtyard to the Casa de la Vall.

like to join in the singing of the National Anthem of Andorra:

El gran Carlemany, mon pare,
dels alarbs em deslliurà,
i del cel vida em donà
de Meritxell la gran Mare.
Princesa nasquí i pubilla
entre dues nacions neutral;
sols resto l'unica filla
de l'imperi Carlemany.
Creient i lliure onze segles,
creient i lliure vull ser.
Siguin els furs mos tutors
i mos Prínceps defensors!

An old "martinet", opposite the Casa de la Vall.

The Casa de la Vall.

The ''Tribunal de Corts'', or Law Courts, at the Casa de la Vall.

THE CASA DE LA VALL

At the end of an attractive steep winding street, leading from the central Plaça de Benlloch, stands the well-known ''House of the Valley'', seat of the government of Andorra. It is an ancient ''pairal'', or ancestral, house, which was privately-owned until 1580. Since then it has belonged to the ''Consell General de les Valls'', the supreme governing body, which holds official ceremonies here.

The Casa de la Vall has the unmistakable appearance of an old fortess. Completely restored, at the front there is a fine Romanesque-like voussoired doorway, over which is the coat of arms of Andorra, featuring a bishop's mitre and crozier, the four bars of Catalonia, three bars and two Bearn cows, and the motto *Virtus unita fortior*. At each corner of this historic building rise war-like turrets. In the rear, there is a voussoired doorway and, in the right-hand corner, a turret with a pyramid-shaped slate roof. In the forecourt there is a large ''martinet'' or trip-hammer, and a sculpture by Viladomat.

A typical Andorran kitchen, in the Casa de la Vall.

THE CHAPEL OF SAINT ERMENGOL

This chapel, dedicated to the patron saint of the diocese and of the Valleys, is where the Councillors attend mass, and communicates directly with the Council Chamber, which contains some interesting 17th-century paintings, and the famous ''Cupboard with Six Keys'', each of whose locks correspond to the keys of the original six municipalities, and in which are kept important documents relating to the history of Andorra. The kitchen, with its huge fireplace, is very interesting. On the floor above, where the members of the ''Consell'' used to sleep,

Andorran handicraft in the museum of the Casa de la Vall.

Old saddles in the museum of the Casa de la Vall.

is now the Museum of Andorran Art and History. A banner and a church candle, the gifts of Napoleon and Pope John XXIII respectively, are displayed in the chapel.

THE CHURCH OF SANT ESTEVE

Standing on one of the intersecting streets of the Plaça del Bisbe Benlloch, this is Andorra la Vella's parish church. Its restoration was directed by Puig i Cadafalch, conserving its original structure and a beautiful 12-century apse adorned with Lombard motifs. The original bell tower, which was seriously damaged by lightning, was later reconstructed in Romanesque style.

The Chapel of Sant Ermengol, in the Casa de la Vall.

The famous ''cupboard with six keys'', in the Council Chamber (Casa de la Vall).

Les Escaldes-Engordany and Andorra la Vella.

SANTA COLOMA

This enchanting little village stretches out along an esplanade, and is overlooked by its church with its venerable Romanesque architecture. The lovely old church contrasts with the modern buildings which surround it, and which are ever increasing in number. The building of the church began at the end of the 10th century, which is when its pre-Romanesque apse may date from. The bell tower and the nave are 12th century. The bell tower, 17.76 metres high, is famous for its cylindrical shape, one of very few of this type in existence. It has four storeys with double windows and a series of Lombard arches, and seems to have been built in two stages, the first, perhaps built over a pre-Romanesque work, responsible for the first two storeys and the second, pure Lombard Romanesque in style, for the upper two. There are, as in the Church of Sant Miquel d'Engolasters, grotesque stone carvings on the capitals.

The church contains a horseshoe arch, leading into the apse. Above this triumphal arch, some 12th-century paintings of the Lamb of God and two angels can still be admired.

Inside the church there is a 60-centimetre high 12th-century carving of the Virgin "del Remei".

The church, with its peculiar design, fits in perfectly with the surrounding countryside, the whole scene being one of Andorra's most characteristic views.

View of Anyós.

ANYÓS

A rustic little village on the left bank of the Valira, sheltered by huge rocks, on which stands the Romanesque Chapel of Sant Cristòfor, dominating the length of a lovely valley.

The chapel was altered in the 16th century, but still conserves its Romanesque apse and the lower part of the north wall. The square bell tower is the only one in Andorra which is situated in the middle of the roof. Inside, there is a late 13th-century French Gothic Last Supper painted on the tambour of the apse. The other paintings are of the 16th century, as is the altarpiece, which is dedicated to Saint Christopher.

SISPONY

A typical Andorran village lying in the Muntaner Valley, near to Pla de la Costa. In Sispony, the ruins of an old Romanesque church can still be seen.

L'ALDOSA

A small village with magnificent views, L'Aldosa has a riding school, and many riding enthusiasts are attracted here.

The Sant
Antoni
bridge over
the River
Valira del
Nord. It is
Andorra's
oldest
bridge,
believed to
go back to
the 11th-
century.

The tunnels at La Massana.

LA MASSANA

The fourth Andorran municipality, situated at an altitude of 1,240 metres. Andorra's two highest mountains, Coma Pedrosa and Pla de l'Estany are to be found in this area. An important tourist centre, La Massana, with its typical houses and modern residential areas, looks down over a splendid valley. The church has suffered many alterations, with the result that its only remaining Romanesque feature is the bell tower, whose roof, strangely, is in the same style as others in the Alt Urgell and Vall d'Aran regions of Catalonia.

The Church at Sant Antoni de la Grella.

La Massana.

A typical house, now
no longer standing,
at La Massana.

Overall view of La
Massana.

The ''Coll de la Botella'', Pal.

A view of La Massana.

Pal, a picturesque spot.

ERTS

An attractive village whose greyish houses provide a striking contrast to the surprising whiteness of the church. From here, a pleasant excursion to the delightful Vall de Setúria can be made.

PAL

An interesting combination of old, renovated, housing and more modern buildings, clustered around the beautiful church of Sant Climent. The most outstanding feature of this Romanesque church is the slenderness of its square, pyramid-roofed bell tower, decorated with Lombard bands on three of its storeys, and with double windows on the top storey. Inside, the most noteworthy features are the remains of some 16th-century frescoes, the altarpiece (1709), a wrought-iron grille, and a statue of the *Mare de Déu del Remei* — a 12th-century polychrome wood carving — and a Romanesque cross, also polychrome.

It should also be mentioned that Pal has excellent ski facilities.

*The Roman-
esque
Church of
Sant
Climent, at
Pal (La
Massana).*

View of Arinsal.

ARINSAL

Situated in the heart of the Setúria Valley, this small village offers the tourist several modern hotels. The church has an interesting bell tower, and contains an 18th- century painting of *la Verge de les Neus* Well-equipped ski facilities, easily accessible, have recently been installed.

Arinsal produces a well-known table water which is particularly appreciated in France and Spain.

The church at Arinsal.

A waterfall near Arinsal.

Arinsal and the river
of the same name.

Arinsal, a village
immortalised in the
book ''Un andorrà
lluny del poble''.

A view of the Ordino Valley.

ORDINO

Situated at the foot of Mount Casamanya, on the top of a strategic hill, at an altitude of 1,304 metres, Ordino, an important centre and the third Andorra municipality, offers splendid panoramic views of its idyllic valley. In former times, it was the municipality of the ''pairal'' houses, belonging to noble families of great wealth obtained from the exploitation of the iron ore mined in the surrounding mountains. To this day, one can see the remains of the forges owned by the Areny-Plandolit and Rossell families, and the ancestral home of ''Don Guillem'', Ordino's powerful iron magnate.

The attraction of the town comes from its irregular plan, with many picturesque and evocative narrow streets flanked by noble houses. Of these, two of the most interesting are that of the Fiter-Riba family, where the well-known Catalan poet Mossèn Jacint Verdaguer lived for a time, and where ancient documents are preserved, and the birth-place of Baron Guillem Areny de Plandolit, author of the ''Nova Reforma'', a house, now converted into a museum, containing an important library and with a beautiful wrought-iron balcony. Its delightful garden is adorned with some artistic wrought-iron *martinets*. In the town square stands the church and the town hall, on whose wall can still be seen the iron ring

LES VALLS D'ORDINO I D'INCLES
SON MÉS PLENES D'HARMONIA,
DE SOMNI I DE MISTERI,
ALS RAÍGS QUE HI DEIXA CAURE
L'HEMISFERI, A LA SERENA
DE QUI COVA EL MÓN.

Mn. CINTO VERDAGUER 1883
DEL POEMA "CANIGÓ"
FESTIVAL HOMENATGE 1961

used to chain wrong-doers thus exposed to public scorn. The church, probably built over another of Romanesque style, was completely reconstructed in the 17th century, and it is not known whether the bell tower belongs to the original church or to the later reconstruction, in imitation of the earlier Romanesque style.

From Ordino, it is possible to make interesting excursions to the ''Meca'' Castle and to the Casamanya Cave.

LA CORTINADA

The former importance of this village close to Ordino is shown by the presence of various aristocratic houses, among which the most interesting is ''Can Pal''.

Also interesting is the 12th-century Romanesque Church of Sant Martí, which was extended in 1630. The bell tower is Romanesque, though the date of its building is difficult to ascertain exactly, and the

The Romanesque Church of Sant Martí, La Cortinada, (Ordino).

View of La Cortinada.

apse is one of the largest in Andorra.

In 1967, some frescoes (late 11th- or early 12th-century), which had been hidden by a vault in a side-chapel, were discovered. Their colours are remarkably vivid and clear, red and ochre dominating on the left-hand side of the chapel, blue and green on the right.

More frescoes were discovered in 1968, this time in the Chapel of Christ. These portray Saint Martin of Tours, patron saint of the church, a dove, a bird of prey, some unidentified figures, and others thought to portray Saint Bricius and Saint Sebastian.

Can Pal, Andorra's oldest house, at La Cortinada.

LLORTS

An attractive medieval village, surrounded by springs rich in ferruginous waters, about three kilometres from La Cortinada, in the middle of surprisingly lovely, ochre-tinted countryside. The ''torrent de Llorts'', which has its source in the Angonella Lakes, irrigates the land, and seems to sing of love in a passionate medieval voice.

Several ancient houses still stand in Llorts, and a church with a double bell gable. Inside, there is a beautiful crucifix, and a Baroque altar, protected by a wrought iron screen.

EL SERRAT

El Serrat is a village high in the mountains, where, coming down from the Tristaina Lakes, (sung of by the great Catalan poet Verdaguer in his poem *Canigó*), two rivers, the Sorteny and the Valira, meet. It has become a popular place for tourists, because of its marvellous scenery and because of its easy access from France by way of the Rat Pass.

Overall view of Llorts.

*The Serrat
waterfall.*

A pleasant spot in El Serrat.

The Margineda bridge, crossing the Gran Valira.

CANÒLIC

This shrine, dedicated to the patron saint of Sant Julià de Lòria, is situated at an altitude of 1,528 metres. The statue of Our Lady of Canòlic was found, as a plaque near the door testifies, in 1223. It presides over the Renaissance-style high altar. A very popular celebration is held around the chapel on the last Saturday of May, when every worshipper, after mass, is given holy bread. Along with the many worshippers who attend, there is at least one member of every family of Sant Julià. A pretty and easily-accessible spot, Canòlic receives many visitors.

Detail of Nagol.

BIXESSARRI

A tiny village of medieval style, where it is forbidden to build houses not conforming to the traditional style of the country, Bixessarri stands on the banks of the River Os. Though the houses in general are attractive, most interesting is "Can Pere", where 16th-century furniture and documents are preserved.

AIXOVALL

Another small village whose attraction for tourists is endorsed by the modern hotels built on the main road. Aixovall has a hermitage dedicated to Santa Filomena.

NAGOL

A rustic village at an altitude of 1,129 metres, surrounded by idyllically beautiful scenery. Nearby, and higher up, is the Chapel of Sant Serni, or Sant Cerní, once the Church of Laurèdia, which, as it was consecrated in 1055, would seem to have its origins in the 11th century.
The scenery is incomparably beautiful, and none other than the bearded Emperor Charlemagne is said to have travelled through it.

The Shrine at Canòlic.
Typical houses at Bixessarri.

12th-century statue of Our Lady of Canòlic, the patron saint of Sant Julià de Lòria.

Camp Ramonet (2,603 metres), at La Rabassa.

CERTERS

A picturesque little village whose houses seem to huddle protectively together. Certers is thought to be one of the oldest populated places in Andorra. Its attraction as a tourist resort has given rise to many modern housing developments, which have given a renewed vigour to the village. From here, a visit to the waterfall at Llumeneres is recommended, where one can also see an ancient mansion and the church built in honour of the *Verge de les Neus*, who once saved the village from an avalanche which threatened it.

EL PUI D'OLIVESA

Made up of two or three ancient mansions where, according to Andorran legend, Charlemagne spent a night on his journey through the country.
The pre-Romanesque Chapel of Sant Mateu, mentioned in a document dated 985 or 986, is worthy of a visit. The floor and the apse are pure Romanesque, though the pointed arch over the doorway was added at a later date.

Mountain refuge, La Rabassa.

Scrambling, one of the many sports popular in Andorra.

Overall view of Sant Julià de Lòria.

The frontier with Spain.

SANT JULIÀ DE LÒRIA

The *Laurèdia* of ancient times, Sant Julià de Lòria was for a long time the most important commercial town of Andorra, and is now an important industrial centre, where the big tobacco factories are based. At an altitude of 909 metres, on the banks of the Valira,this is the nearest town to France. It is the sixth Andorran municipality, a prosperous town which has grown enormously over recent years, but which has retained the peculiar characteristics so typical of Andorran towns and villages. Many tourists visit the town every year.

The church of Sant Julià and Sant Germà is of great interest. Partially Romanesque, restored in 1941, in the interior there is a 68-centimetre high Romanesque statue of the Virgin.

The age-old history of the town has been proved by the Roman and Iberian coins which have been found in the area.

AIXIRIVALL

A small village, just above Sant Julià de Lòria, in the Sibos Forest, now becoming a tourist centre through the building of holiday bungalows.

JUVERRI

A delightful village, now surrounded by holiday residences, whose historic buildings cluster around its Romanesque church.

AUVINYÀ

A picturesque village lying near to the 10th-century pre-Romanesque Church of Sant Romà, which was completely restored in 1963. The modern housing has been cleverly designed to blend in with the beautiful surroundings. Not far away is the densely wooded area of the great La Rabassa Forest.

FONTANEDA

This village, lying on the slopes of the "serra del Teix" belongs to the municipality of Sant Julià de Lòria. Its old houses with their artistic balconies and the charming rustic church stand out amongst the typically Andorran architecture of the village.
Between Fontaneda and Sant Julià de Lòria there are the ruins of the ancient Pui d'Olivesa Castle and of "La Seca".

Tobacco fields.

MAS D'ALINS

A lovely spot four kilometres from Fontaneda. The little Church of Sant Esteve, wholly Romanesque in style, contains an altar stone, also Romanesque, kept under the present wooden altar.
Not far away is the attractive Les Pardines farm, which commands beautiful panoramic views.

Tobacco, the basis of agriculture and industry in Andorra. ▷

THE SNOWS OF ANDORRA

The beautiful Principality of Andorra enjoys the privilege of being ideal for both winter and summer tourism. In winter, the snow-capped mountains are a delight to contemplate from the villages of the valleys.

But the snows of Andorra, apart from their aesthetic value, also make winter sports possible, to the extent that Andorran is well-known all over the world as a skier's paradise. There are modern ski-lifts, and excellent, well-equipped natural slopes, which make taking part in winter sports a real pleasure. Another of Andorra's winter attractions is mountaineering. There are many local climbers, and many more come from other countries.

View of the Envalira Valley, with the "Cercle dels Pessons" in the background.

Lake ''Els Pessons''.

A snow-covered
Andorra la Vella.

Views of El Pas de la Casa.

Andorra is a real skiers paradise.

ANDORRAN LEGENDS

Andorrra is a world of poetry, of dream-like landscapes, and of charming deeply-rooted popular traditions, a world full of imagination, possessing a rich store of enchanting legends. Two of the most beautiful of these refer to Lake Engolasters. According to one, sooner or later all the stars in the sky will become trapped in the bosom of its waters, attracted by the bewitching beauty of the lake. The other tells the story of how the lake came to be. It was formed by a great flood, the punishment for the lack of charity of a woman from a nearby village. She had refused a poor pilgrim a piece of bread, the pilgrim turning out to be none other than Christ.

Another popular story is that of the fighters of Setúria. The shepherds of Os, in Spain, and those of the Andorran village of La Massana, both claimed ownership of the pastures of Setúria, and decided to settle the dispute in combat. The Andorrans won the fight, and, consequently, the lands. Another legend is that of the ''Serra de l'Honor'', a tale of the fights of Louis the Pious with the Arabs. The Christian monarch won victory by appealling to the honour of his soldiers, who, stirred by his words, swept to victory. But perhaps the most romantic and fantastic of Andorran legends is the story of the first Andorran man and woman, she the daughter of a powerful king. Her beauty and goodness were only surpassed by that of her mother, who was, unfortunately, dead. The king married again, this time a woman whose beauty was only matched by her wickedness. One of her first acts was to order the death of the princess, but the ruffians given this order could not bring themselves to carry it out, and abandoned her in desolate spot. Her nurse, however, fearing the worst, had kept constant watch, and seeing that the men had left her, went to her, where they embraced pitifully, before taking flight. They finally came to an enchanting place close to the River Valira, called the ''Toll de la Senyoreta'', in what was then Laurèdia, where they made a hut of of stones and branches to protect them from wild animals.

One morning, the princess was washing in the crystal waters of the Valira, when she came across a man, badly wounded and unconscious on the shore of the ''Toll''. She called to her nurse, and they carried him into the hut and cared for him until he was well. The young man was astonished when he recognised the princess, for he was one of the leaders of the rebels against the despotic queen of her father's kingdom. Having lost the battle, he had been miraculously saved. Despite the difference in rank, the princess, now known as the ''Dama Blanca'' for the constant vigil she keeps over Andorra, appreciating the great qualities of body and mind and the goodness of the avenger of her people, fell in love with and married him, and they became Andorra's first couple, their children populating the entire area of the Valleys, conserving and propagating the virtues of the princess and the hero to this very day.

''The biggest, highest, most rugged mountains ever seen ...'' ▷

View of Soldeu.

The ski resort at Soldeu-El Tarter. ▷

SOLDEU

Situated 1,825 metres above sea-level, one of the highest populated points in Europe, Soldeu is almost permanently surrounded by a lovely snow-covered landscape. Another of its natural charms is the many-hued forest around it.

Despite its high altitude, Soldeu enjoys a rather mild climate, which makes it a perfect spot for the ski resort built there. It has an excellent mountain hotel, three modern ski-lifts and a chair-lift which can, in just minutes, transport tourists and skiers 450 metres up to the magnificent Pla dels Espiolets, with its superb views over the Pyrenees and its many carefully-prepared ski slopes.

The Romanesque
Church of Sant Joan
de Caselles, covered
by snow.

The ski slopes at
Arcalís.

Dawn over the Tristaina Lakes, of which there are three, as their name indicates ("tri stagna").

ANDORRA COIN
ISSUES

St. Ermengol five-peseta piece (1977)

Gold sovereign (1978)

Gold sovereign (1980)

Gold sovereign (1981)

Silver 25-pence piece (1984)

Cupronickel 2-pence piece. Nature
Conservation Series (1984)

Reproduced are some of the coins
issued in recent series by the Co-
prince the Bishop of Urgell. We hope
they are of interest.

ESCUDO DE ORO, S.A. COLLECTIONS

ALL SPAIN

1 MADRID
2 BARCELONA
3 SEVILLE
4 MAJORCA
5 THE COSTA BRAVA
8 CORDOBA
9 GRANADA
10 VALENCIA
11 TOLEDO
12 SANTIAGO
13 IBIZA and Formentera
14 CADIZ and provincia
15 MONTSERRAT
17 TENERIFE
20 BURGOS
24 SEGOVIA
25 SARAGOSSA
26 SALAMANCA
27 AVILA
28 MINORCA
29 SAN SEBASTIAN and Guipúzcoa
30 ASTURIAS
31 LA CORUNNA and the Rías Altas
32 TARRAGONA
40 CUENCA
41 LEON
42 PONTEVEDRA, VIGO and Rías Bajas
43 RONDA
46 SIGUENZA
47 ANDALUSIA
52 EXTREMADURA
54 MORELLA
58 VALLDEMOSSA

GUIDES

1 MADRID
2 BARCELONA
3 LA RIOJA
4 MAJORCA
6 SANTIAGO DE COMPOSTELA
7 SEVILLA
8 ANDALUCIA
9 GRAN CANARIA
12 GALICIA
13 CORDOBA
14 COSTA BLANCA
15 GRANADA
22 SEGOVIA
25 AVILA
26 HUESCA
28 TOLEDO
30 SANTANDER

———————————

4 LONDON

———————————

1 LA HABANA VIEJA
2 EL CAPITOLIO (CUBA)

ALL EUROPE

1 ANDORRA
2 LISBON
3 LONDON
4 BRUGES
6 MONACO
7 VIENNA
11 VERDUN
12 THE TOWER OF LONDON
13 ANTWERP
14 WESTMINSTER ABBEY
15 THE SPANISH RIDING
    SCHOOL IN VIENNA
17 WINDSOR CASTLE
18 LA CÔTE D'OPAL
19 COTE D'AZUR
22 BRUSSELS
23 SCHÖNBRUNN PALACE
25 CYPRUS
26 HOFBURG PALACE
27 ALSACE
28 RHODES
30 CORFU
31 MALTA
32 PERPIGNAN
33 STRASBOURG
34 MADEIRA + PORTO SANTO
35 CERDAGNE - CAPCIR
36 BERLIN
42 CONFLENT-CANIGOU

TOURISM

1 COSTA DEL SOL
2 COSTA BRAVA
3 ANDORRA
4 ANTEQUERA
6 MENORCA
8 MALLORCA
9 TENERIFE
14 LA ALPUJARRA
15 LA AXARQUIA
16 PARQUE ARDALES AND EL CHORRO
17 NERJA
18 GAUDI
19 BARCELONA
21 MARBELLA
23 LA MANGA DEL MAR MENOR
25 CATEDRAL DE LEON
26 MONTSERRAT
34 RONDA
35 IBIZA-FORMENTERA
37 GIRONA
38 CADIZ
39 ALMERIA
40 SAGRADA FAMILIA
42 FATIMA
43 LANZAROTE
44 MEZQUITA HASSAN II
45 JEREZ DE LA FRONTERA
46 PALS
47 FUENGIROLA
48 SANTILLANA DEL MAR
49 LA ALHAMBRA Y EL GENERALIFE
51 MONACO-MONTECARLO

ALL AMERICA

1 PUERTO RICO
2 SANTO DOMINGO
3 AREQUIPA
4 COSTA RICA
6 CARACAS
7 LA HABANA
8 LIMA
9 CUZCO

ALL AFRICA

1 MOROCCO
3 TUNISIA

ART IN SPAIN

1 PALAU DE LA MUSICA CATALANA
2 GAUDI
3 PRADO MUSEUM I
   (Spanish Painting)
4 PRADO MUSEUM I
   (Foreing Painting)
5 MONASTERY OF GUADALUPE
7 THE FINE ARTS MUSUEM OF SEVILLE
10 THE CATHEDRAL OF GIRONA
11 GRAN TEATRO DEL LICEO
   (Great Opera House
14 PICASSO
15 ROYAL PALACE OF SEVILLE
19 THE ALHAMBRA AND THE GENERALIFE
21 ROYAL ESTATE OF ARANJUEZ
22 ROYAL ESTATE OF EL PARDO
24 ROYAL PALACE OF SAN ILDEFONSO
26 OUR LADY OF THE PILLAR OF
   SARAGOSSA
27 TEMPLE DE LA SAGRADA FAMILIA
28 POBLET ABTEI
29 THE CATHEDRAL OF SEVILLE
30 THE CATHEDRAL DE MAJORCA
32 MEZQUITA DE CORDOBA
33 GOYA
34 THE CATHEDRAL OF BARCELONA
35 CASA - MUSEU CASTELL GALA-DALI
   PUBOL
36 THE CATHEDRAL OF SIGUENZA
37 SANTA MARIA LA REAL DE NAJERA
38 CASA - MUSEU SALVADOR DALI
   PORT LLIGAT

MONOGRAPHS (S)

5 SOLAR ENERGY IN THE CERDAGNE
10 MORELLA
20 CAPILLA REAL DE GRANADA
31 CORDILLERAS DE PUERTO RICO
38 GIBRALTAR
50 BRUGES
68 MONASTERIO DE PIEDRA
70 TORREVIEJA
74 VALLDEMOSSA
75 ANTWERP
84 CATHEDRAL OF MAJORCA
85 CATHEDRAL OF BARCELONA
86 VALL D'UXO

MONOGRAPHS (L)

5 PUERTO RICO
6 THE OLD SAN JUAN
9 THE CITY OF BRUGES
19 MURALLAS DE SAN JUAN

MAPS

1 MADRID
2 BARCELONA
6 LONDON
8 ALICANTE
20 PANAMA
31 SEVILLE
33 BRUGES
36 SEGOVIA
37 CORDOBA
38 CADIZ
40 PALMA OF MAJORCA
45 JEREZ DE LA FRONTERA
47 AVILA
48 ANDORRA
50 SALAMANCA
52 LEON
53 BURGOS
58 IBIZA
78 GRANADA
80 MONACO
93 MENORCA
94 LA MANGA DEL MAR MENOR
96 COSTA BRAVA
97 LLORET DE MAR
98 SANTANDER

Protegemos el bosque; papel procedente de cultivos forestales controlados
Wir schützen den Wald. Papier aus kontrollierten Forsten.
We protect our forests. The paper used comes from controlled forestry plantations
Nous sauvegardons la forêt: papier provenant de cultures forestières contrôlées

Text, photographs, lay-out, design and printing by
EDITORIAL ESCUDO DE ORO, S.A.
Rights of total or partial reproduction and translation reserved.
Copyright of this edition for photographs and text:
© EDITORIAL ESCUDO DE ORO, S.A.
The publishers would like to thank AVIOTEC for providing
the aerial photographs on pages 32, 33, 34 and 38.
13th Edition - I.S.B.N. 84-378-0273-3
Dep. Legal. B. 18824-1999

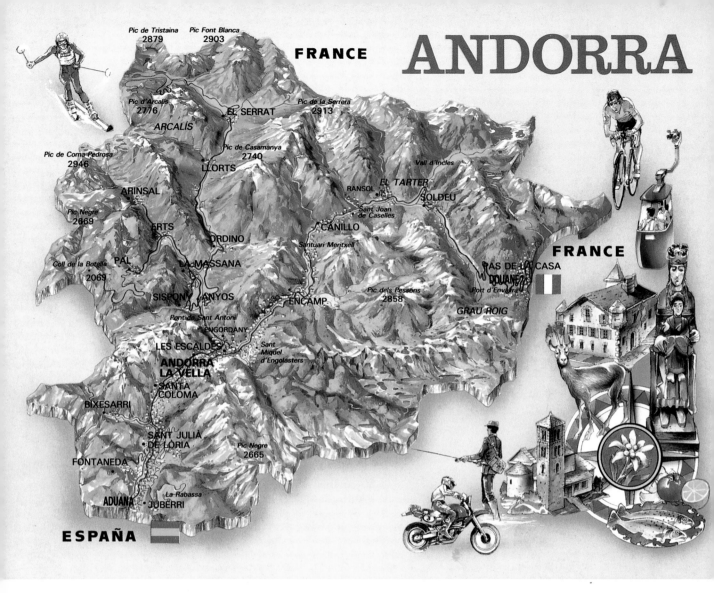

ANDORRA

Pic de Tristaina 2879
Pic Font Blanca 2903
FRANCE
Pic d'Arcalís 2776
EL SERRAT
Pic de la Serrera 2913
ARCALÍS
Pic de Coma Pedrosa 2946
Pic de Casamanya 2740
LLORTS
Vall d'Incles
RANSOL
EL TARTER
SOLDEU
ARINSAL
Sant Joan de Caselles
Pic Negre 2669
ERTS
ORDINO
CANILLO
Santuari Meritxell
PAL
LA MASSANA
Coll de la Botella 2069
FRANCE
SISPONY ANYOS
ENCAMP
Pic dels Pessons 2858
PAS DE LA CASA
DOUANE
Pont de Sant Antoni
ENGORDANY
Port d'Envalira
LES ESCALDES
Sant Miquel d'Engolàsters
GRAU ROIG
ANDORRA LA VELLA
SANTA COLOMA
BIXESARRI
SANT JULIÀ DE LÒRIA
Pic Negre 2665
FONTANEDA
La Rabassa
ADUANA JUBERRI
ESPAÑA

Contents